MW00366876

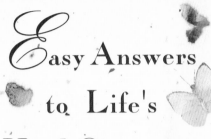

Easy Answers to Life's Hard Questions

By Lynne Ames

Illustrated and designed by
Kerren Barbas

PETER PAUPER PRESS, INC.
WHITE PLAINS, NEW YORK

Copyright © 1999
Peter Pauper Press, Inc.
202 Mamaroneck Avenue
White Plains, NY 10601
All rights reserved
ISBN 0-88088-392-8
Printed in China
7 6 5 4

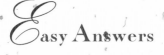

Easy Answers

to Life's

Hard Questions

A friend's secret

is a precious gift;

once entrusted to you,

it must be kept

forever.

*L*ook back

to where

you have been

for a clue to where

you will be going.

Marry someone

whose soul you love.

Passion fades,

but friendship remains

forever.

*I*n an argument,
a cool head will soothe a
raging heart most
effectively.

*W*orry enough to anticipate trouble, but not so much as to bring it about.

Cut your losses quickly

if you make a mistake.

Tell yourself,

"I am human, I can err,"

and then move on.

*T*rue friendship

is a fabric that nothing

can unravel.

Holidays are the

dessert in the meal of

life—

enjoy them

to the last calorie.

*M*elt the

icy fingers of fear

with the sunshine of hope.

✦

A true friend

never sits in judgment.

*T*reat your memories
like a movie reel:
rewind and savor
the good scenes;
speed through those that
caused you pain.

The lonely heart
finds love in
unlikely places.

✦

Anger is a flame
that leaves nothing
but ashes.

*L*ove drives us.

Whether for a man or a

woman, a parent or a child,

a place or an ideal, love

energizes virtually all

human activity.

Step by gentle step,

you can overcome the

greatest sorrow.

✦

Every love

is unique.

Pure joy is as rare

and as fleeting

as a wisp of fog.

Break a promise

to a friend, and you've

lost something irreplaceable

within yourself.

$\mathcal{H}$ome is that place

where you feel

most safe.

✦

$\mathcal{S}$ometimes, tact

is needed when telling

the truth.

Everyone asks for advice, but few listen.

Marriage is a contract

written in the ink

of passion, respect, and

compromise.

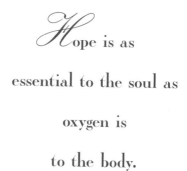

*H*ope is as

essential to the soul as

oxygen is

to the body.

When life becomes overwhelming, go to a small quiet corner of your mind and remember happier times.

Even if you can't forget a hurt, you can forgive the person who delivered it.

The sweetest

grapes are picked

from the vineyard of

friendship.

The monster of
despair thrives on
solitude; your sorrows
will shrink as soon as
you share them
with someone.

$\mathscr{G}$ossip is like a river:

it can always be traced

back to its source.

You may find it is

easier to forgive

someone her

weaknesses than her

strengths.

A jealous friend

is the most dangerous

enemy.

There is no viable
alternative to growing old,
so we might as well do it
with grace and grit.

Generosity is more
a matter of mood than
money; listen with
gentle patience to a
friend in need and you
bestow a gift
greater than gold.

*B*ase your

self-image on one

person's opinion—

your own.

You cannot always

change circumstances, but you

can always change your

reaction to them.

$\mathcal{A}$n insecure person

will soak up

flattery like a sponge.

If life hands you
a bitter pill, it may
turn out to be the
very medicine that
will make you strong.

A tattered well-read paperback is worth more than an unopened gold-bound volume.

$\mathcal{E}$laborate ritual

is no substitute

for faith.

*H*aving money

allows you to live as

plainly as you choose.

If anything in nature

strikes you as ugly,

you are not appreciating

its diversity.

The flower of
romance grows best in
the soil of good
conversation.

Unfortunately,

virtue may command

admiration but not

always affection.

*G*uilt is what we feel

when we have

injured others;

shame, when we

have embarrassed ourselves.

$\mathcal{S}$ave the life

of a helpless animal,

and you have done

the work of God.

*Forgive yourself first.
Only after you have
allowed yourself
freedom from your own
regrets can you let go of
grudges toward others.*

*A*dmit your weaknesses,

and you are halfway to

conquering them.

✦

A mirror is only as good

as the reflection in it.

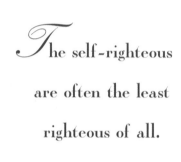

The self-righteous are often the least righteous of all.

If everybody

says you're wrong,

you just might want

to reconsider.

If you are lost,
remember—you have merely
taken a detour on the way
to your destination.

The river of time

flows at its own

unchangeable pace,

even under the bridge

to the Millennium.

The safety net of
friendship will catch
you when you fall.

hen we

sympathize with someone,

we know; when we empathize,

we understand.

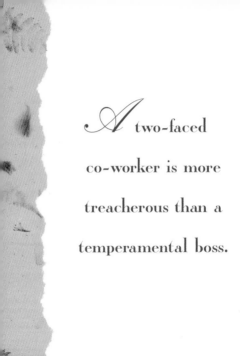

$\mathscr{A}$ two-faced

co-worker is more

treacherous than a

temperamental boss.

A mother nurtures

her child long past

childhood.

✦

*W*ork is only one

part of life.

Beauty feeds the eye

but does not necessarily

nourish the soul.

✦

The stars shine brightest

in the darkest night.

If your neighbor's

lawn seems greener

than yours, look at it

when the sun has set.

$\mathcal{I}$ was annoyed when someone bumped into me on the street, until I turned and saw that he was blind.

One warm exchange of
words with a pleasant
stranger can light up
an entire day.

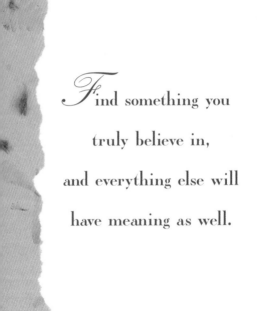

$\mathcal{F}$ind something you

truly believe in,

and everything else will

have meaning as well.

In the throes of

indecision, a deep,

inner voice will

whisper an answer.